Y-Mee's A B C Book of Emotions

By Wanda M. Argersinger

© 2008 L-Bow

L-B✳W

www.L-Bowonline.com

ISBN 978-0-615-26401-1

In memory of, and thanks to, all the patients who live on a daily basis with chronic illnesses. Your stories and lives and the way you live them were the basis for the tongue-in-cheek advice contained within this book.

Thank you to my parents, Tom and Joyce, for allowing me to be who I am, idiosyncrasies and all, and loving me as I am. You are always *there*, and for someone who lives with chronic illness everyday, *there* can be a lot. I love you.

If Patch Adams and Erma Bombeck had had a baby, it surely would have been Wanda Argersinger. Though gifted with a magnificently, magnified sense of humor Wanda is no stranger to suffering. She has lived with Lupus for 12 years. She has personally experienced the highs and lows that come from having a chronic illness. She has learned that laughter IS the best medicine. She writes hilarious anecdotes about real life meat and potatoes. Anecdotes (also antidotes) that counter act the toxins from negative thinking. Having been privileged to be on Wanda's e-mail list, I get to read her work early, fresh off the brain. I always feel lifted after opening my email and finding another of Wanda's life experiences causing me to laugh out loud, chuckle or gently giggle within. I have often thought that if I were ill or depressed and I had a choice between a prescribed medication that usually comes with a second medication to counter act the first medication's side effects or a prescription for anything that Wanda has written, I would hope that the doctor knows how to spell Wanda's name correctly. Wanda has an innate understanding of how humor chemically stimulates healing in the mind body. Now with the creation of her Y-Mee dolls and the hilariously, healing words that accompany them, you can experience simple joy, while learning about emotions that we all experience. I regularly tell my client's that the more senses that they are able to utilize while solving a dilemma, the greater their success will be. Whether it's pain control, depression, grief and loss, the aftermath of divorce or even chronic illness, humor is always a beneficial part of the healing process.

Wanda has a gift for turning the ordinary and the mundane into something fun and comical. Who would have thought that a question mark could take on the life of the Y-Mee doll? The Y-Mee dolls and the writings that accompany them are wonderfully therapeutic tools that promote healing the mind body and the heart and spirit. You can't overdose on them and they have no side effects. You can also hug it when the going gets tough. It's a pleasant reminder that bad feelings don't last forever. I recommend a Y-Mee doll to anyone who is dealing with dis-ease, no matter the diagnosis or dilemma. So buy one, beg one, borrow one or steal one (please be kind and return it so the owner will have it when their emotions are adrift). Get your Y-Mee doll so that the next time you ask," why me', you will find a smile begin to creep across your face.

Beverly L. Copeland, MS, LMHC

Contents

A is for Anger!

Y-Mee's definition:

A circular emotion according to the dictionary. Anger means to make angry; angry means to show anger. Anger spreads from one person to another just by being in the same proximity of the person who is angry. Anger is wasted energy, wasted emotion, wasted time.

Y-Mee's Advice:

Suggestions have been made that when angry a person should count to 10, and if very angry, count to 100. Y-Mee says forget the numbers. With the memory lapses you have, you probably can't count to 100 anyway. Don't try beating the object of your anger either. Chances are, before you could get to the object, you would have 1) forgotten why you were angry in the first place, 2) exhausted yourself trying to walk that far, 3) stopped to pick daisies on the way.

Anger:_____

_____

_____

_____

_____

_____

_____

_____

_____

_____

_____

_____

_____

_____

B is for Bored!

Y-Mee's definition:

Boredom is for wimps and wooses. How can anyone be bored when there are fabulous shows on the television such as the myriad of judges who are willing to sell their opinions for our amusement? Or shows such as Jerry Springer? If television is not your cup of tea, and you can get out of the house, you can always go to the local mall and watch real people for amusement.

Y-Mee's Advice:

Get a book. Get a television. Get a telephone. Get a telescope to spy on your neighbors. Sit on your front porch and watch the plants grow. Excitement is everywhere. Open your eyes and find it.

Boredom:_____

_____

_____

_____

_____

_____

_____

_____

_____

_____

_____

_____

_____

_____

_____

_____

C is for Confused!

Y-Mee's definition:

Confused can also be defined as any sentence that begins with What, Where, When or Why followed by AM I or DID I? (as in, What did I come in this room for?)

Y-Mee's Advice:

For a few rare people, organization helps relieve the state of being confused. For the rest of us, being confused is our normal state. Y-Mee says – "don't fight it". It's not a bad place to live as you will have plenty of company there.

Confusion:_____

_____

_____

_____

_____

_____

_____

_____

_____

_____

_____

_____

_____

_____

_____

_____

_____

_____

_____

_____

_____

_____

_____

_____

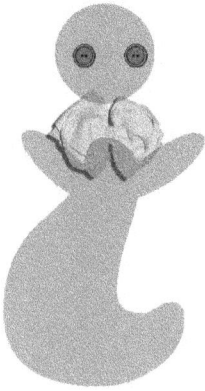

D is for Depressed!

Y-Mee's definition:

An illness that involves the body, mood, and thoughts, that affect the way a person eats and sleeps, the way one feels about oneself, and the way one thinks about things. Sounds like life to Y-Mee. Illness or loss can be depressive or lead to depression. Come to think of it mirrors could be termed depressive as they certainly lead to depression.

Y-Mee's Advice:

Cover the mirrors. Hide your skinny jeans and forget about them. Spend your money on great makeup and jewelry. Lock your significant other in a closet. Eat the ice cream. If you're going to be depressed, you might as well look good and eat what you like.

Depressed/Depression:_____

_____

_____

_____

_____

_____

_____

_____

_____

_____

_____

_____

_____

_____

_____

_____

E is for Exhausted!

Y-Mee's definition:

Beyond tired. Beyond worn out. At the point that just lifting your head from the pillow is an expenditure of energy you feel you don't have. There is no energy to walk. There is no energy to talk. There is no energy to do anything. There is no energy in your body. This can occur for any number of reasons, or it is how you can feel for no reason at all. Exhaustion has its own life but can be caused by great expenditures of energy, or can come from emotional upheaval. It can be more psychological than physical – but is real none the less. You may feel it certain times of the day – like in the morning when you first get out of bed, mid-morning, noon time, mid-afternoon, evening and, at night when the day has been too much and it's time to go to bed.

Y-Mee's Advice:

Try to determine why you are exhausted. If your exhaustion is for physical reasons, you need to rest. If your exhaustion is psychological you need to get moving. If you have exhausted yourself doing things, stop doing them. If your exhaustion is from doing nothing, find out if there is a medical reason. Exhaustion is not a normal state for normal people. Being crabby, grumpy, bitchy, sarcastic, and even mean are normal states of being for some people, but exhaustion is not.

Exhaustion:_____

_____

_____

_____

F is for Frustrated!

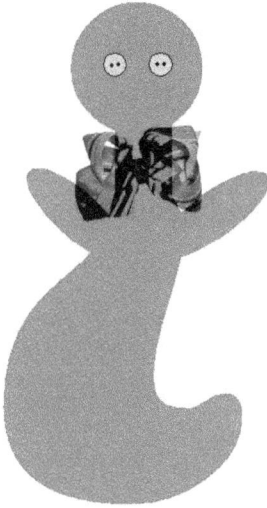

Y-Mee's definition:

How you feel when you try or want to do any and everything and fail. These things include sleeping, waking, moving, walking, thinking, remembering, going, coming, speaking, shopping, cooking, writing, reading, cleaning, and sometimes just plain being. Frustration can also be experienced when you are taking diuretics, are in unfamiliar places and can't locate the bathroom.

Y-Mee's Advice:

Don't fret about it. Use it to your advantage. When people ask you why you're in a bad mood, tell them you're frustrated because you can't

_____ (fill in the blank.)

Hopefully they will feel sorry for you and do the task you wanted done. Caution: Don't waste this opportunity on the little things. THINK BIG. (Ex. I'm frustrated because I know I'll never be able to go to Hawaii.)

Frustration:_____

_____

_____

_____

_____

_____

_____

_____

_____

_____

_____

_____

_____

_____

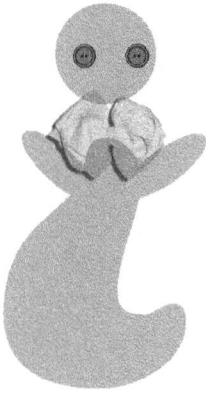

G is for Grateful!

Y-Mee's definition:

Appreciating the good things in our lives. And yes, no matter what happens in our lives there are always good things. Sometimes we have to dig beneath the dust, or walk outside to see them, but they do exist.

Y-Mee's Advice:

No matter how bad we perceive our situation to be, there are always things to be grateful (thankful) for. Family, friends, physicians, and pharmaceuticals are just a few that come to mind. If your good things don't include people or possessions among the things you count as good – you can always resort to buying good things – like chocolate, ice cream, jewelry, purses and shoes.

Gratefulness:_____

_____

_____

_____

_____

_____

_____

_____

_____

_____

_____

_____

_____

_____

H is for Happy!

Y-Mee's definition:

Happy is like the feeling you got when you were a child and ran through spring rain, played in mud puddles, stayed up late in the summer, swam naked in the lake, got real mail and packages delivered to your door, believed in The Tooth Fairy, Santa Claus and that the moon was made of green cheese. It's a feeling you may come close to feeling now when your grandchildren give you butterfly kisses, or you indulge and have an ice cream cone in summer and let it drip down your hands.

Y-Mee's Advice:

If you're happy, enjoy it. If you're not happy, find a child and play their games for

just a while. Make up stories to share.
Doodle on the good paper with the pens
you've been saving.

Happy:_____

_____
_____
_____
_____
_____
_____
_____
_____
_____
_____
_____
_____
_____
_____
_____

I is for Irritated!

Y-Mee's definition:

How we feel for any number of reasons, such as when other people don't understand how we feel, when annoying drivers won't get out of our way, when the grocery store has run out of chocolate ice cream, when we want to read and our significant other wants to talk, when we want to talk and our significant other wants to watch television, how we feel when we want to shop and our bank account screams no. Irritation can also be felt for no particular reason at all, especially if you are female. Also can be how we feel when we have to go to and / or wait for another doctor, or add yet another medicine to our arsenal.

Y-Mee's Advice:

Listen up – IT IS NOT THEIR PROBLEM.
People who don't have the illnesses we deal
with, or tragedies we experience, will never
understand how we feel. Sometimes we
don't understand how we feel, or why we
feel a certain way. We can't control the
other people in our lives, we can only
control ourselves. Well most of the time we
can control ourselves. Don't waste your
precious energy on a useless emotion. Eat
chocolate instead. At least you'll feel better.

Irriatation:

J is for Jubilant!

Y-Mee's definition:

Much like having a jubilee. Something to be celebrated. Even the crabs have a jubilee every now and then. Why should we be any different? (Ok, so many crabs are caught and eaten because they jubilee, but that doesn't stop the other crabs from having a jubilee again.) Don't let the little ups and downs of life stop you from feeling jubilant about your accomplishments.

Y-Mee's Advice:

If you have a difficult time thinking of some reason to be jubilant, open your eyes. There is a great big world full of exciting things.

Or look inside yourself. We all have reasons to feel triumphant or satisfied for something we have done, or overcome, or helped another person successfully do.

Jubilation:_____

_____

_____

_____

_____

_____

_____

_____

_____

_____

_____

_____

_____

_____

_____

_____

_____

_____

K is for Krazy!

Y-Mee's definition:

The magic ingredient to a survivable life. Anything taken too seriously can damage your aura, your spirit, your essence, your dreams, your health, your inner child, your life.

Y-Mee's Advice:

Aim for being at least a little bit krazy everyday. Without kraziness, boredom sets in. Kraziness can be found everywhere if a person keeps an open mind, open eyes, and a willingness to enjoy the things that are out of the norm. Laughter and kraziness go hand in hand.

Kraziness:_____

_____

_____

_____

_____

_____

_____

_____

_____

_____

_____

_____

_____

_____

_____

_____

_____

L is for Lonely!

Y-Mee's definition:

The act of being or feeling alone. Imagined or real – not a good way to feel.

Y-Mee's Advice:

This is the most difficult emotion to deal with. There is no one to blame. No one to take revenge upon. No one to be angry with. Bottom line – there is no one. Get out and find someone. Join a book club, a garden club, a volunteer club, a parachuting club, a hot air balloon club. Go to a bookstore, a library, a coffee shop, the mall, a church. Join any and every club you have an interest in. Volunteer at a hospital, a school, a nursing home. If you can't get out, get started on the telephone. Become the person who calls others to check on them. Become the person who calls others to remind them of upcoming meetings. Become the voice on the 1-900 phone line and earn a little money. People are everywhere and just waiting to make new friends.

Loneliness:_____

_____

_____

_____

_____

_____

_____

_____

_____

_____

_____

_____

M is for Mad!

Y-Mee's definition:

That feeling of being fired up, hot, and ready to pounce on whatever or whomever caused us to feel this way. How we feel when things don't go our way. How we feel when someone crosses over one of our emotional barriers. How we feel when faced with injustice. How we feel when we think we have been left out or forgotten. How we feel for any number of real or imagined situations.

Y-Mee's Advice:

First – always determine, to the best of your ability, if the cause of the MAD you are feeling is real or imagined. Many times we find that our MAD is unjustified and caused by our imagination. We create our own injustice and, thus, our own state of being MAD. If the MAD is justified, don't try to get even, at least not right away. Remember. Take your time to plan your revenge. Time makes the plan better, and many times just devising the plan and envisioning the results is so much better than implementing the plan. Imagination is not illegal, so you can feel free to imagine the best revenge ever. Time also allows you to forget what or who made you mad, thus, making revenge unnecessary.

Mad:_____

_____

_____

_____

_____

_____

_____

_____

_____

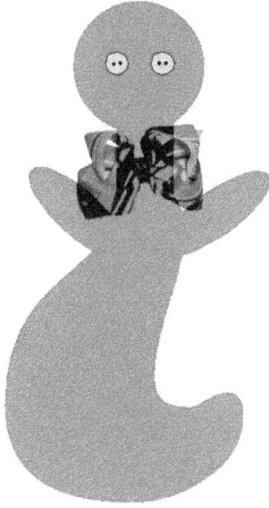

N is for Nervous!

Y-Mee's definition:

That sneaky little feeling that creeps in to the pit of your stomach that makes you speak too fast, laugh too much, twist your hair, click your nails, smack your gum, hyperventilate and / or faint. Everyone has felt nervousness at some time in their life.

Y-Mee's Advice:

Enjoy the butterflies in the stomach. The only thing close to the feeling of nervousness is having your belly button kissed from the inside, and frankly, I'm not sure that's possible.

Nervous:_____

_____

_____

_____

_____

_____

_____

_____

_____

_____

_____

_____

_____

_____

_____

_____

_____

_____

_____

_____

_____

_____

_____

O is for Oh God !

Y-Mee's definition:

The emotion often felt and uttered in that split second when one realizes they should not have hit the send button, mailed the letter, spoken the words, worn the wrong bra, or used liquid dish soap in the dishwasher. This emotion can also be associated with the feelings experienced when a person is told they must have one more medical test, give one more presentation, or bake one more dozen of anything for the party tomorrow.

Y-Mee's Advice:

Breathe deep. Think of the worst that can happen as a result of what you just did and multiply that by a quadrillion. Now you're prepared to face your particular Oh God situation. Either that, or you can join the Foreign Legion and hope no one finds your forwarding address.

Oh God !_____

_____

_____

_____

_____

_____

_____

_____

_____

_____

_____

_____

_____

_____

_____

_____

P is for Pissed off!

Y-Mee's definition:

What happens when a person messes with someone's mind, possessions, habits, personal space, or logic. Not to be confused with the emotion that begins with an A. Pissed Off is an emotion that often ends when one person has physically beaten the crapola out of the person who did the messing

Y-Mee's Advice:

If you are the one who caused another to be Pissed Off and have yet to feel the physical wrath, Y-Mee suggests you run, and run very, very fast. If you have already felt the wrath, see the emotion that begins with O for more help.

Pissed off !_____

_____

_____

_____

_____

_____

_____

_____

_____

_____

_____

_____

_____

_____

_____

_____

_____

Q is for Quixotic!

Y-Mee's definition:

Foolishly impractical. No more explanation needed.

Y-Mee's Advice:

Try to be as quixotic as much as you can and as often as you can.

Quixotic:_____

_____

_____

_____

_____

_____

_____

_____

_____

_____

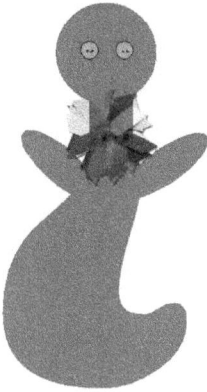

R is for Restless!

Y-Mee's definition:

An emotion most often connected with night time. Usually prevents sleep and also causes the sleeping partner to either endure the tossing and turning or move to another room. May also cause midnight raids on the refrigerator or the pharmaceutical supply.

Y-Mee's Advice:

Always keep a good book handy to read when you can't sleep. If the restlessness is such that you must move constantly, try churning ice cream. At least you'll have something wonderful to eat as a result of your spent energy.

Restless:_____

S is for Stressed!

Y-Mee's definition:

Something that exists but can't harm you without your imagination. It is not the actual stressor that can harm us but rather it is how we deal or not deal with the stressors that become our undoing. Stress can make you feel sick, make you hide, incapacitate you, and even kill you IF YOU let it. Stress can come from work, family, the weather, electronic devices, clocks, cars, other drivers, annoying voices – real or imagined, or from inside yourself. YOU own your stress as what stresses you may be nothing to another person.

Y-Mee's Advice:

Exercise. Listen to soothing music. Play racquet ball and imagine your stressor is the ball and every time you whack the ball you are killing the stressor. (This is extremely effective and safe if your stressor is another person.) Go shopping. Go gardening. Go walking. Do anything physical except beating your stressor. Remember, you own your stressor and can fire it anytime you want. Learn to recognize your stressors and how they make you feel. As soon as you are able to do that YOU CONTROL YOUR STRESSORS

Stressed:

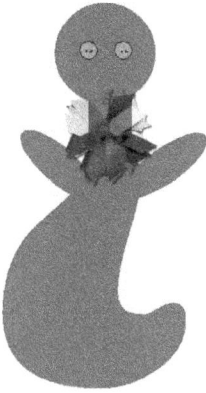

T is for Tired!

Y-Mee's definition:

Tired is the little brother of exhaustion. Though he most often comes before exhaustion, in the twisted world of emotions, he is the little brother. He does the dirty work for his big brother by wearing you down so exhaustion can take over. Most days he shows up before you even get out of bed. He puts his traps out and hopes to ensnare you. The traps can be as simple as dust on a table, a full trash can, dirty clothes in a pile, a smudge on a window or a crooked carpet. Be careful. Try not to be ensnared in his traps, as once in there you are sure to meet his big brother soon.

Y-Mee's Advice:

Get used to it. There are always going to be things that make you tired. You can try to avoid them. You can try to hide from them. You can even try to hire someone to take care of the things that make you tired. But, there will always be another something waiting to zap you, causing you to fall victim to tiredness. If you aren't tired now, you eventually will be.

Tired:_____

_____

_____

_____

_____

_____

_____

_____

_____

_____

_____

_____

U is for Upset!

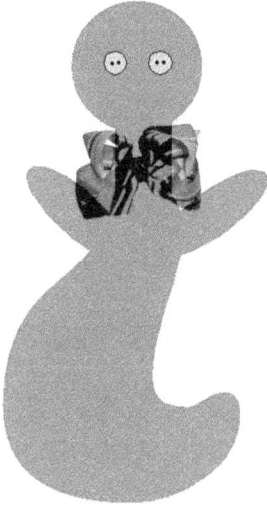

Y-Mee's definition:

Not the kind of upset you feel when milk is spilled, but the upset feeling that makes you cry, or you feel in the pit of your stomach. Often felt when others don't understand how you feel or why you feel the way you do. Can also be felt when the one person in the world you count on to understand, reacts in a way you didn't expect, or didn't want, or don't understand. Upset can be rational or irrational. Either way you own it. Fortunately, upset is one of those feelings that doesn't last very long and is often replaced with a smile or a laugh.

Y-Mee's Advice:

Realize that you can't control others; You can only try to control yourself. It's ok to be upset. It's ok to cry. Your feelings are real. Just don't stay upset. If possible, explain to the person who upset you, what they said or did and how it made you feel. In most cases they have no idea the effect their words or actions have on you. Forgive whoever upset you and forgive yourself. Eat chocolate. Eat ice cream. Paint with finger paints. Go shopping. Call a friend and whine. Move on with your life.

Upset:_____

_____

_____

_____

_____

_____

_____

_____

_____

_____

_____

V is for Vexed!

Y-Mee's definition:

Irritated, distressed and annoyed. Can be for any reason or for no reason at all, or for any imagined reason you can come up with. Often vexed at your significant other just for breathing the air around you.

Y-Mee's Advice:

Breathe. Chant. Walk in the garden. Listen to the birds. Throw stones in the pond. Water something as water is soothing. Water your significant other if they really deserve it.

Vexed:

W is for Wonderful!

Y-Mee's definition:

How you feel when your medications are working. How you feel when you get to do what you want to do. How you feel when the sun shines. How you feel when you can eat chocolate cake without guilt.

Y-Mee's Advice:

Enjoy all the wonderful you can get. It is often short lived, and visits infrequently. If it doesn't come often enough, make your own wonderful by baking brownies and eating as many as you want. Watch every sunset you can. Enjoy a gentle breeze and the feel of it on your skin. Watch the sun set. Listen to the music of your soul. Wonderful is all around if we take the time to become aware of just how much wonderful there is in our lives.

Wonderful:_____

_____

_____

_____

_____

_____

_____

_____

_____

_____

_____

_____

_____

_____

_____

_____

_____

_____

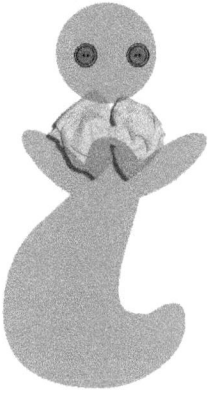

X is for eXactly as you want to feel !

Y-Mee's definition:

How you feel on those rare days when you actually feel like you. You have energy, dreams, desires, and everything seems right in your world.

Y-Mee's Advice:

Enjoy! Revel in the moment! Do the things you want to do and not the things you think you should do or feel you have to do. Be you! The best you can be and enjoy every moment of this special but rare day.

eXactly:_____

_____

_____

Y is for You!

Y-Mee's definition:

Absolutely fandamtastic, unique, one of a kind, never been one like it before, and will never be one like it again - YOU!

Y-Mee's Advice:

Be YOU. Be Younique (unique). Enjoy your fabulosity, your foibles, your laughter, your tears, your gifts, your flaws, your individuality, your love, your beauty, your spirit. Indulge YOU when you can. You are truly a gift.

You: _____

_____

_____

_____

_____

Z is for Zealous !

Y-Mee's definition:

Finally! The end of the alphabet – the end of the book. I'm feeling quite zealous at this moment. It means I can go back to feeling all of the other emotions a-y.

Y-Mee's Advice:

Whenever you experience any of the emotions mentioned in this, all too short, but hopefully funny book, remember what Y-Mee says – it won't last forever. You will soon find yourself feeling something new and different from a different letter of the alphabet. Life is a wonderful, crazy, unexpected, absolutely fantastic ride. Enjoy every moment, no matter what emotion you're feeling.

Zealous:_____

_____

_____

_____

_____

_____

_____

_____

_____

_____

_____

_____

_____

_____

_____

_____

_____

_____

_____